W9-AIJ-311

I'LL FLIP YOU FOR IT, BEETLE BAILEY

by Mort Walker

ACE TEMPO BOOKS, NEW YORK

BEETLE BAILEY: I'LL FLIP YOU FOR IT
Copyright © 1972, 1973, 1974, 1975, 1976, 1977 by King Features Syndicate, Inc.
All rights reserved. No part of this book may be reproduced in any form or by
any means, except for the inclusion of brief quotations in a review, without
permission in writing from the publisher.

An Ace Tempo Original

ISBN: 0-448-16861-8

This Printing: August 1982

Tempo Books is registered in the United States Patent Office

Published simultaneously in Canada

Manufactured in the United States of America

I'LL FLIP YOU FOR IT, BEETLE BAILEY

© King Features Syndicate, Inc.— 1975, World rights reserved.

© King Features Syndicate, Inc., 1975. World rights reserved.

© King Features Syndicate, Inc., 1975. World rights reserved

10-27

HEY! THAT LOOKS LIKE A NEW PENCIL DOWN THERE

I GET YOU, BEETLE! I GET YOU!!

YOU CAN EAT AT THE PX IF YOU DON'T LIKE MY COOKING!!

MORT WALKER

© King Features Syndicate, Inc., 1975. World rights reserved.

© King Features Syndicate, Inc., 1975. World rights reserved.

© King Features Syndicate, Inc., 1975. World rights reserved.

© King Features Syndicate, Inc., 1975. World rights reserved.

TAKE THAT SILVER SERVICE AWAY BEFORE THE INSPECTOR GENERAL ARRIVES

YES, SIR

11-21

I WOULDN'T W
HIM TO GET T
IMPRESSION
PUTTING C
AIRS

© King Features Syndicate, Inc. 1975. World rights reserved.

© King Features Syndicate, Inc., 1978. World rights reserved.

11-29

MORT WALKER

11-27

© King Features Syndicate, Inc., 1975. World rights reserved.

© King Features Syndicate, Inc. 1975. World rights reserved.

12-15

A BEAUTIFUL DIVING CATCH, BEETLE!

TOO BAD YOU SLID INTO LT. FUZZ'S FLOWER BED, THOUGH

MORT WALKER

12-17

© King Features Syndicate, Inc., 1975. World rights reserved.

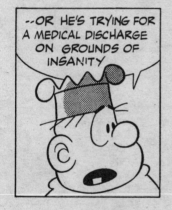

© King Features Syndicate, Inc., 1976. World rights reserved.

1-7

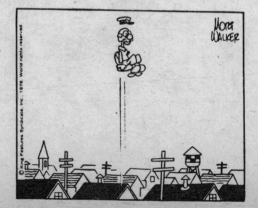

3-16

© King Features Syndicate, Inc., 1976. World rights reserved.

WHY DO YOU
DO THAT?!

© KING Features Syndicate, Inc., 1976.

JUST BECAUSE
IT'S THERE

OTTO

MORT
WALKER